THE CHARLIE BROWN COLLECTION™

CONTENTS

ISBN 0-634-03085-8

HAL•LEONARD®
CORPORATION

7777 W. BLUEMOUND RD. P.O. BOX 13819 MILWAUKEE, WI 53213

Visit Hal Leonard Online at
www.halleonard.com

BASEBALL THEME

CHRISTMAS IS COMING

CHRISTMAS TIME IS HERE

THE GREAT PUMPKIN WALTZ

LINUS AND LUCY

RED BARON

SCHROEDER

SKATING

BASEBALL THEME

By VINCE GUARALDI

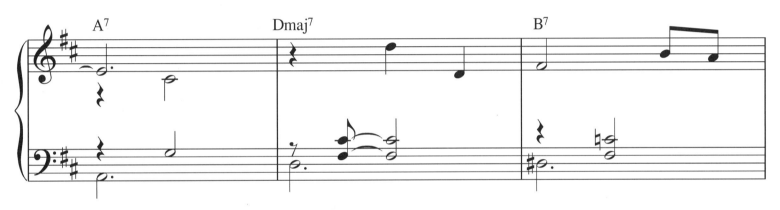

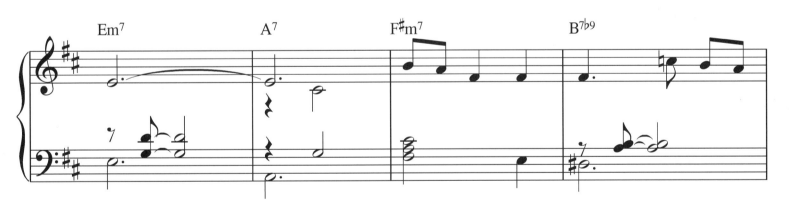

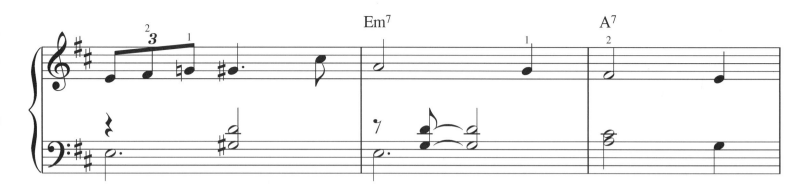

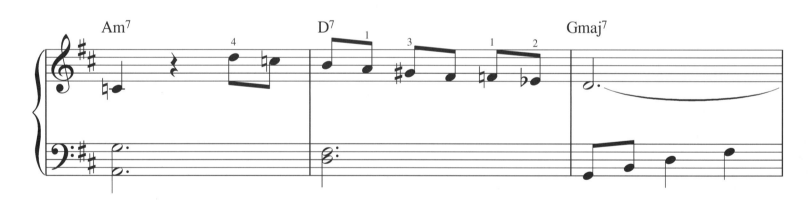

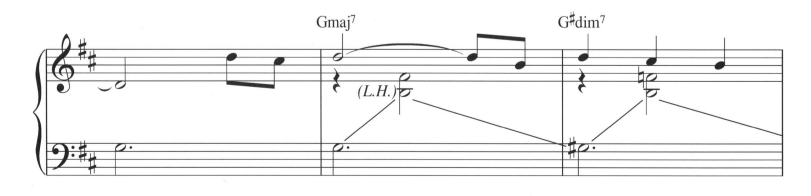

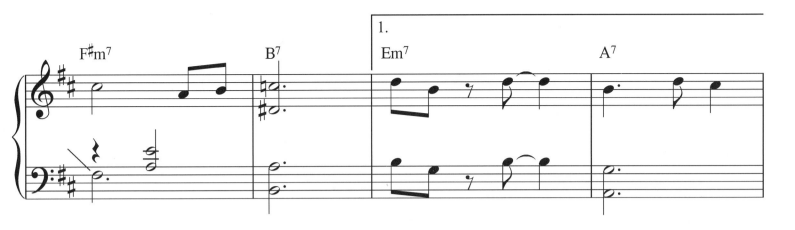

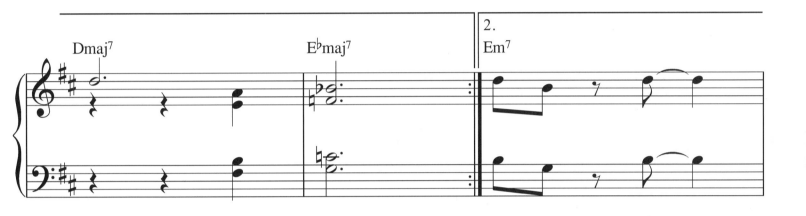

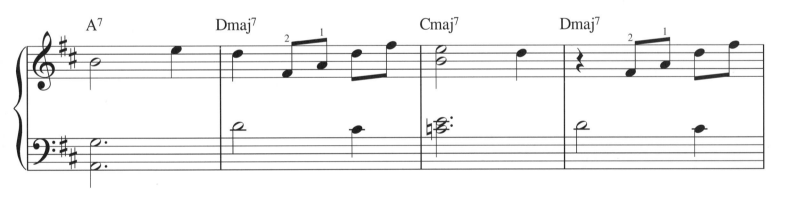

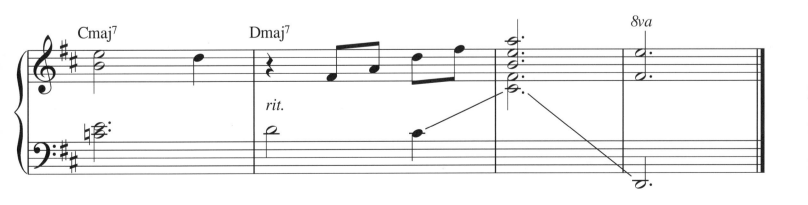

BLUE CHARLIE BROWN

By VINCE GUARALDI

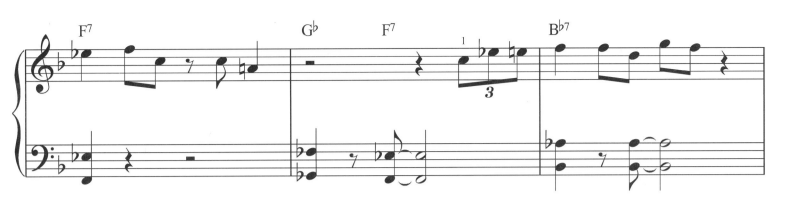

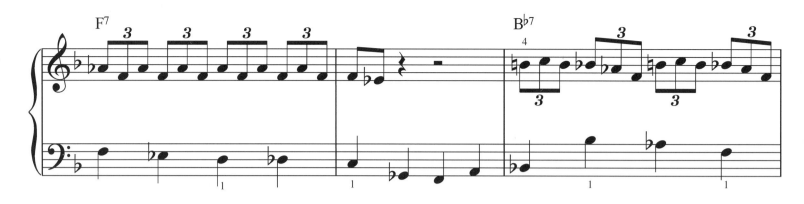

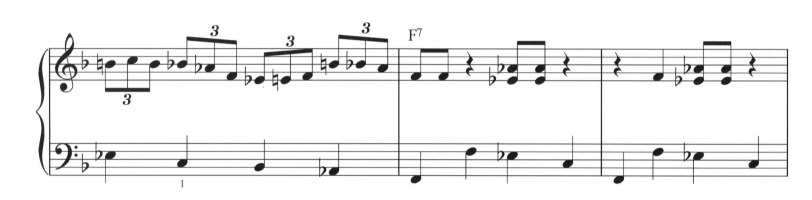

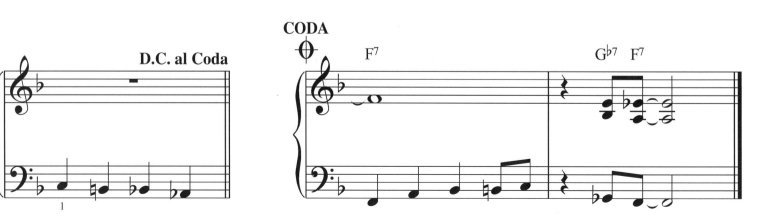

CHARLIE BROWN THEME

By VINCE GUARALDI

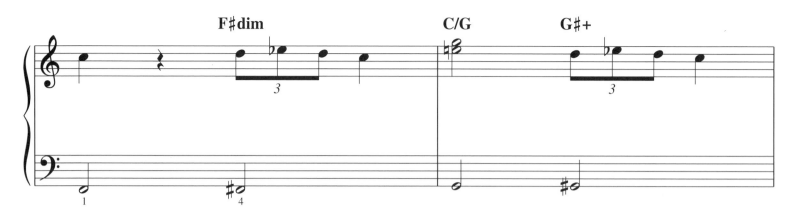

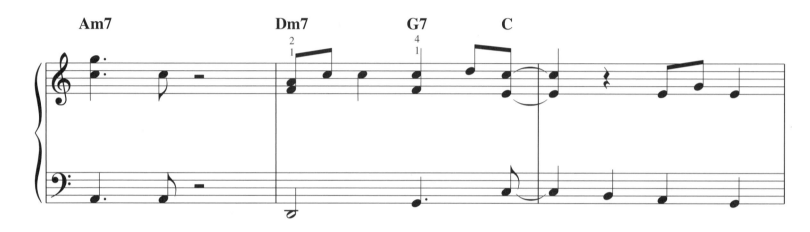

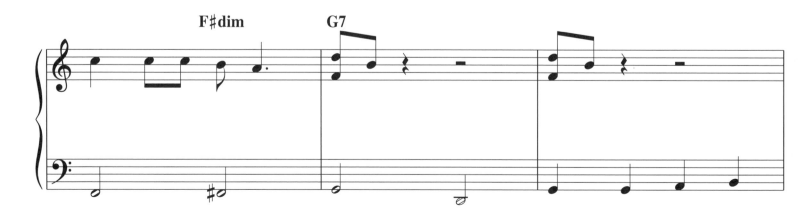

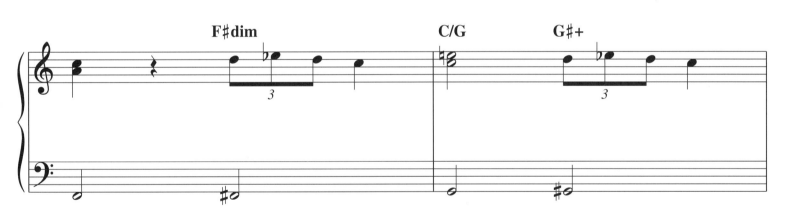

CHRISTMAS IS COMING

By VINCE GUARALDI

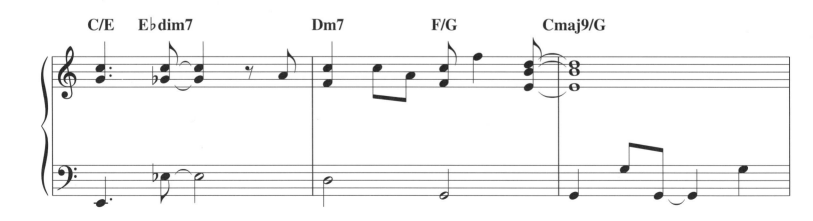

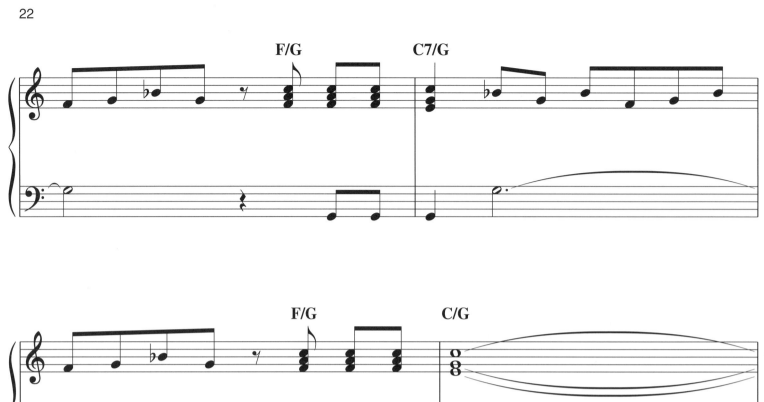

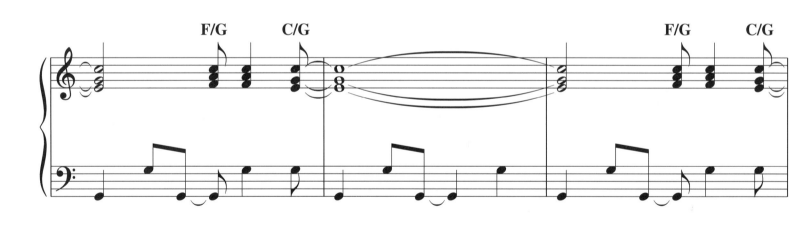

THE GREAT PUMPKIN WALTZ

By VINCE GUARALDI

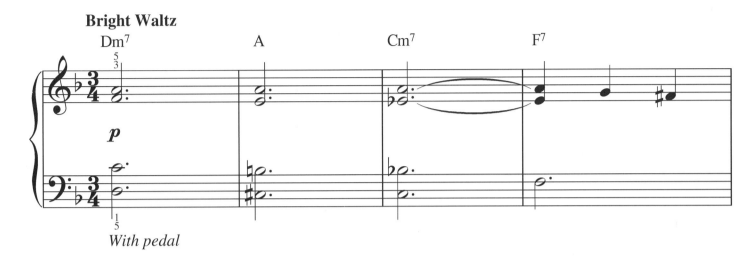

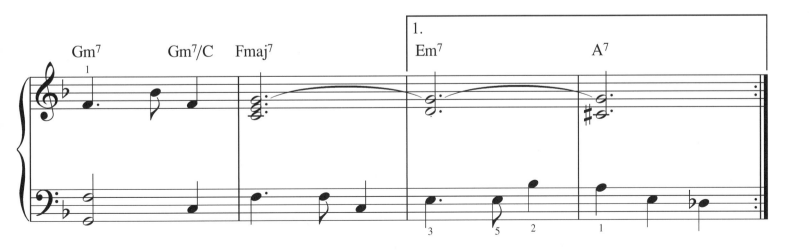

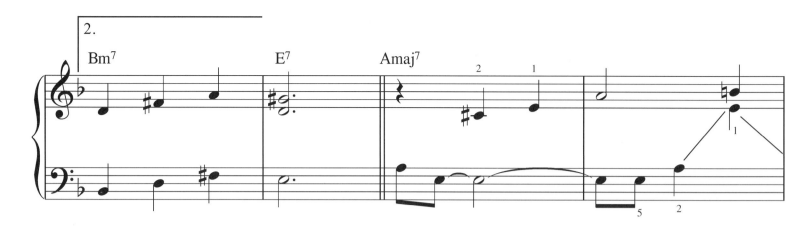

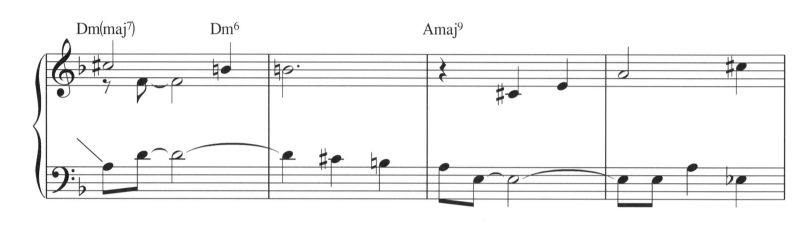

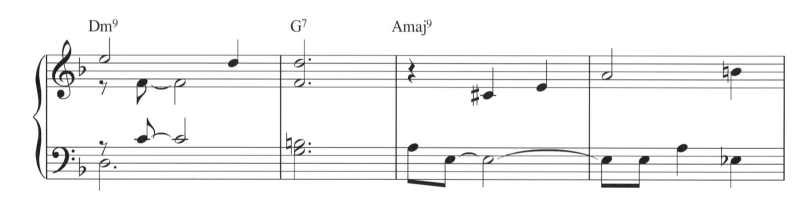

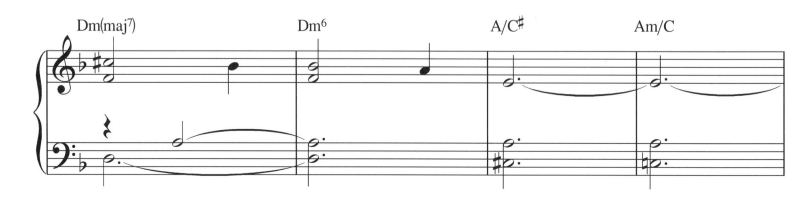

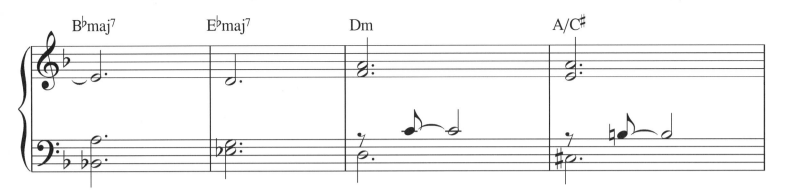

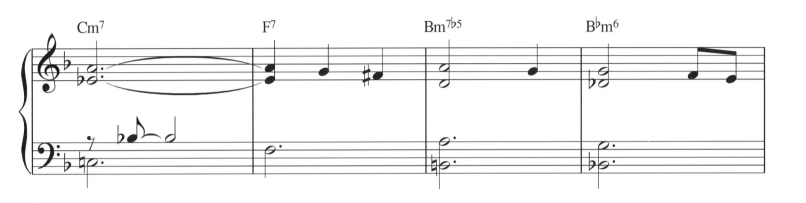

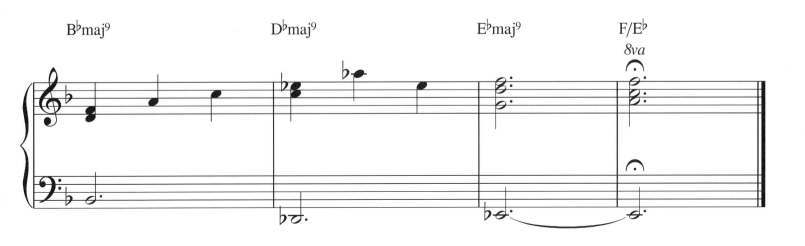

CHRISTMAS TIME IS HERE

Words by Lee Mendelson
Music by VINCE GUARALDI

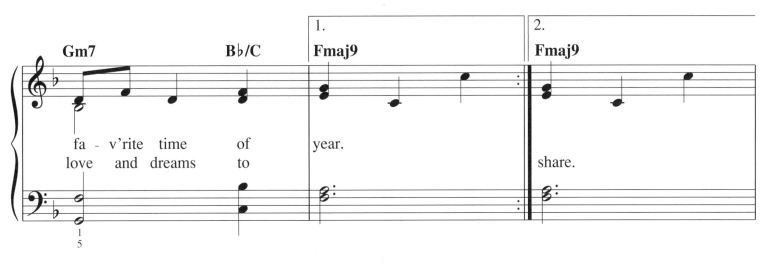

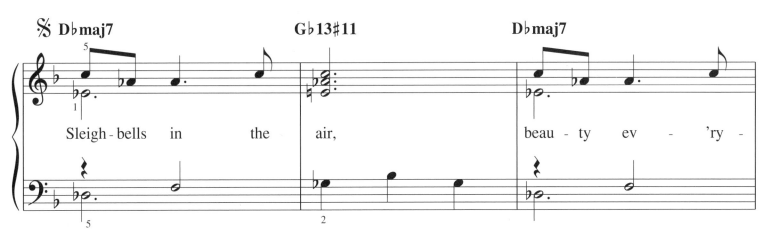

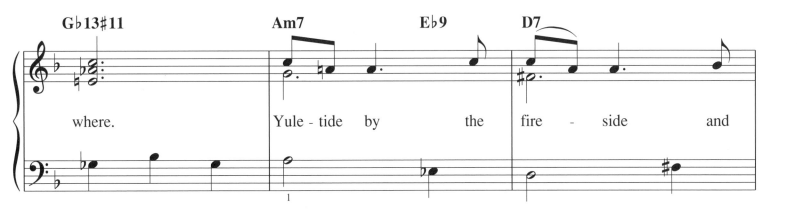

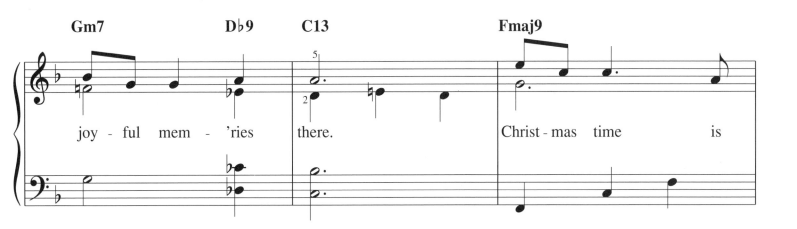

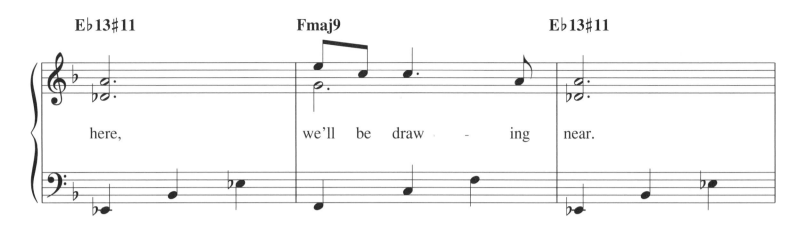

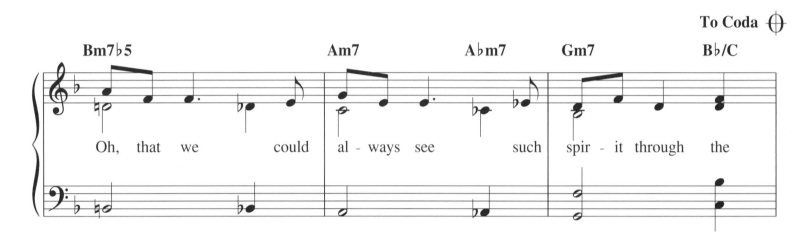

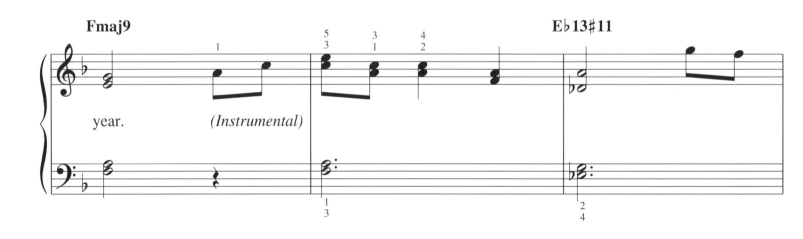

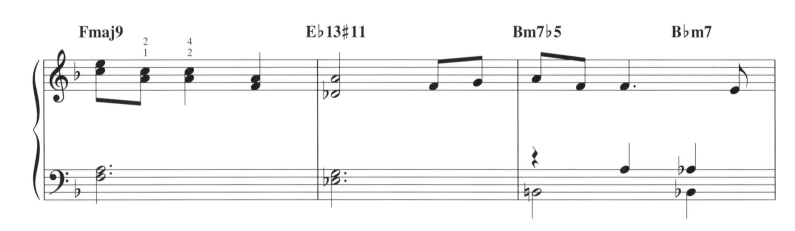

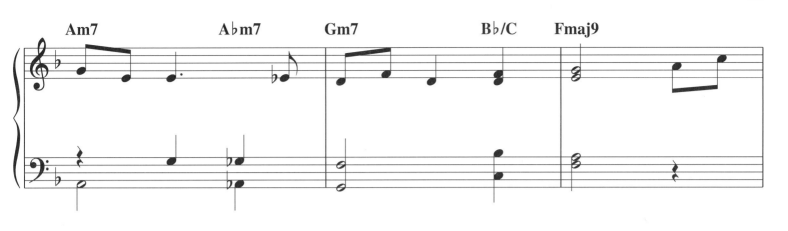

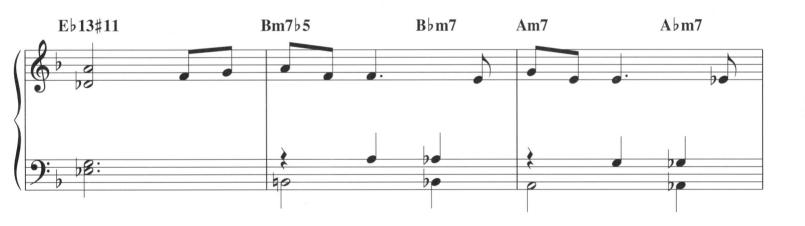

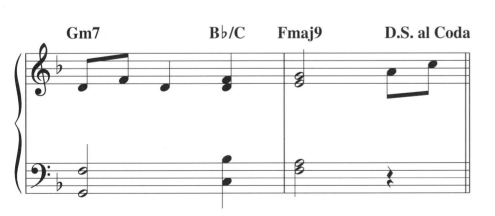

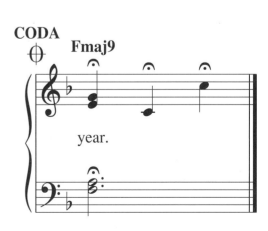

HAPPINESS THEME

By VINCE GUARALDI

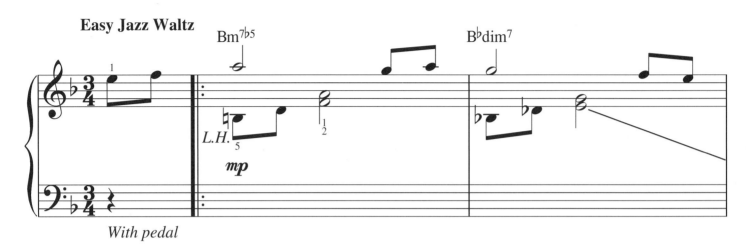

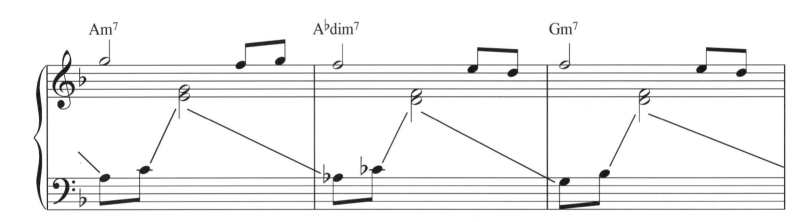

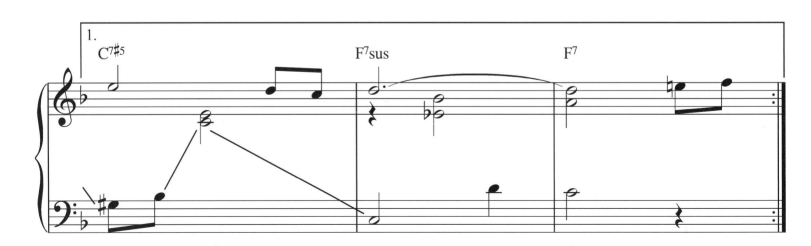

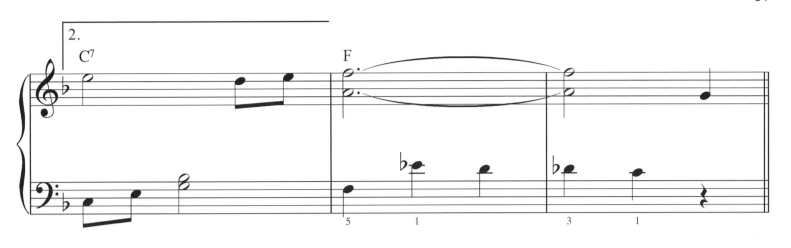

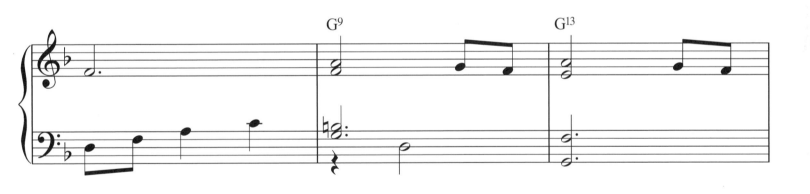

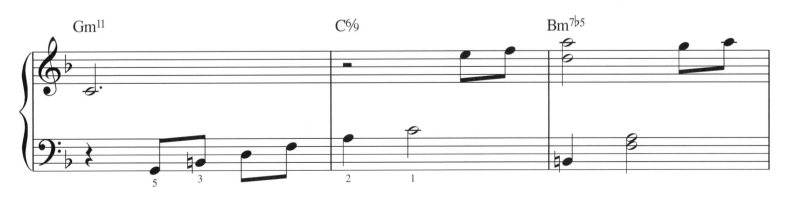

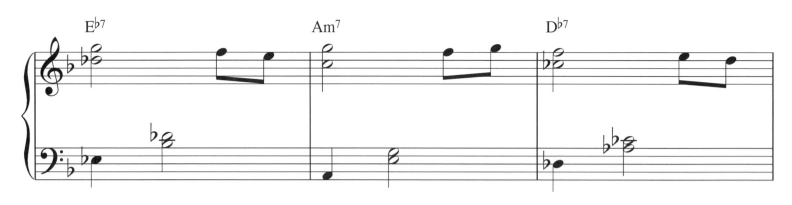

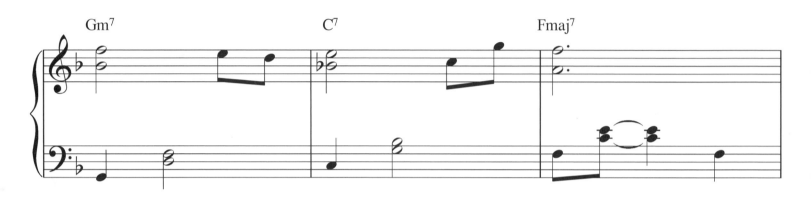

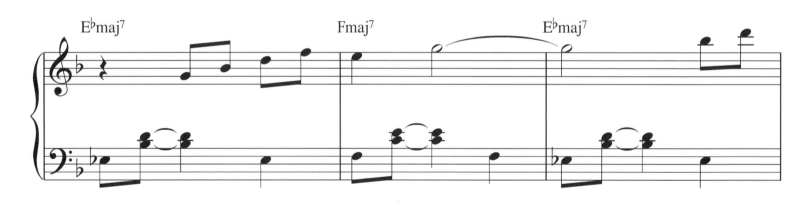

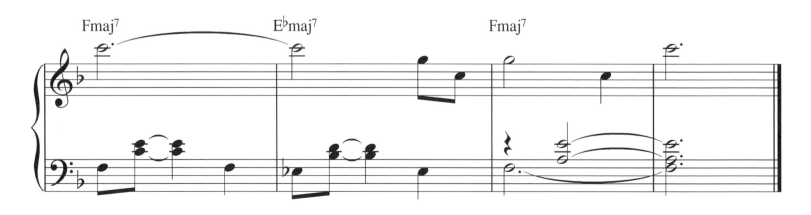

JOE COOL

By VINCE GUARALDI

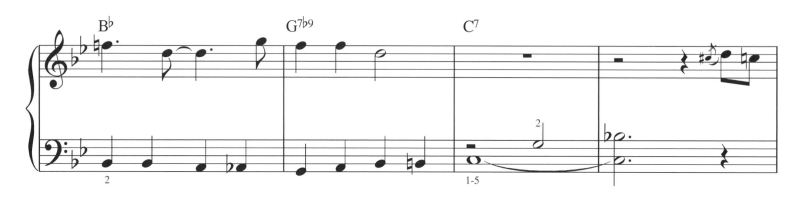

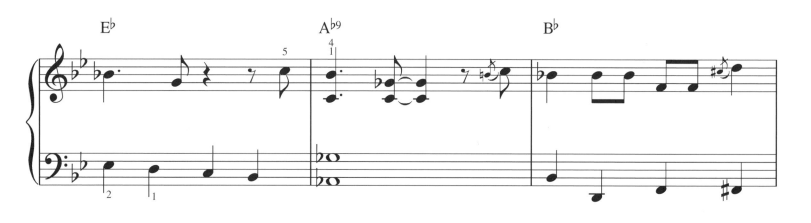

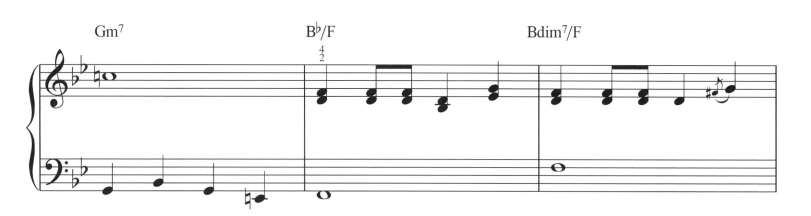

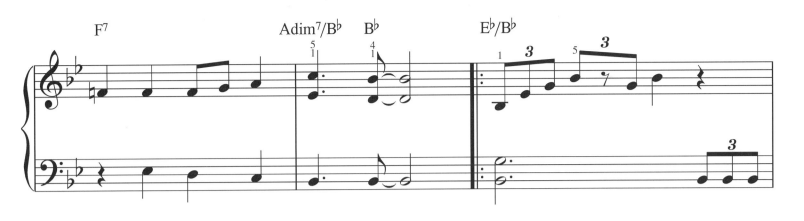

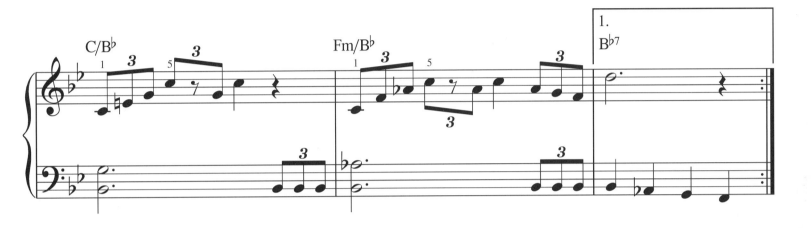

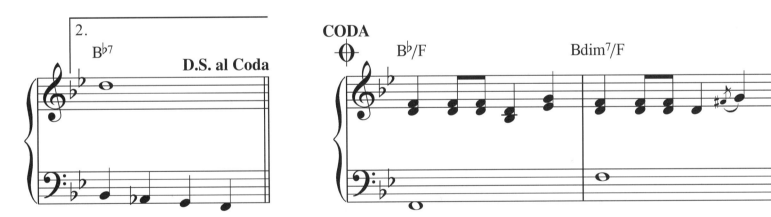

HE'S YOUR DOG, CHARLIE BROWN

By VINCE GUARALDI

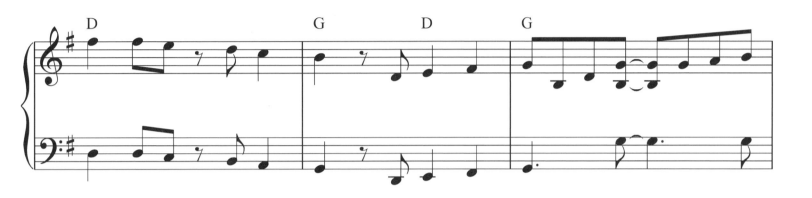

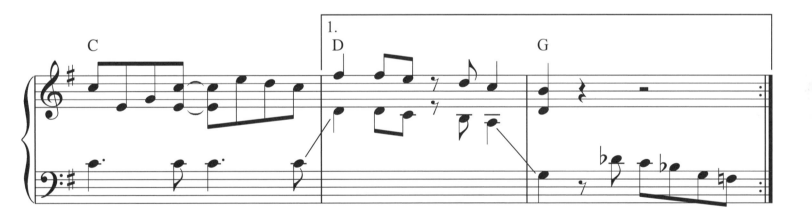

LINUS AND LUCY

By VINCE GUARALDI

LOVE WILL COME

By VINCE GUARALDI

Slowly, with feeling

With pedal

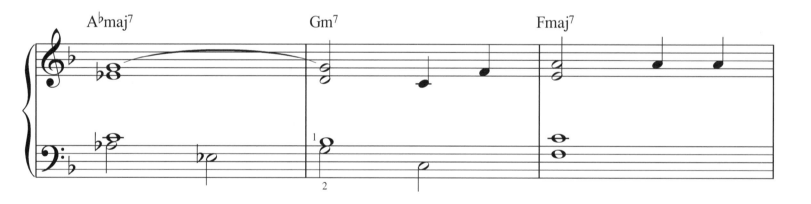

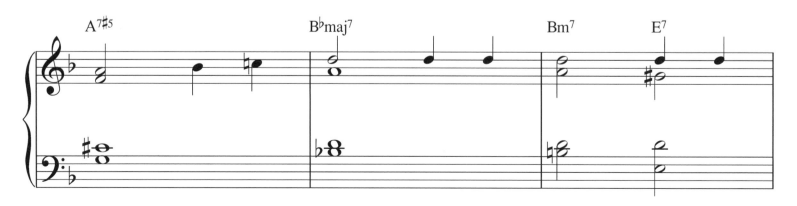

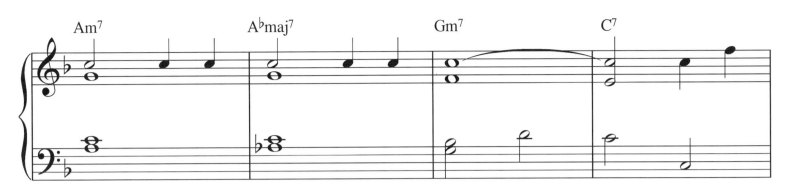

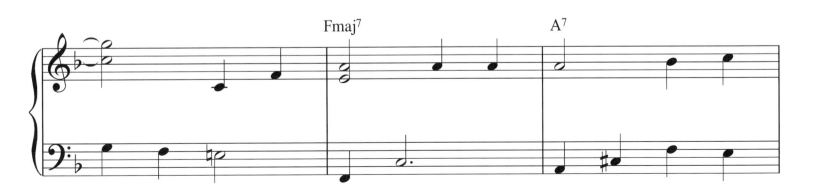

44

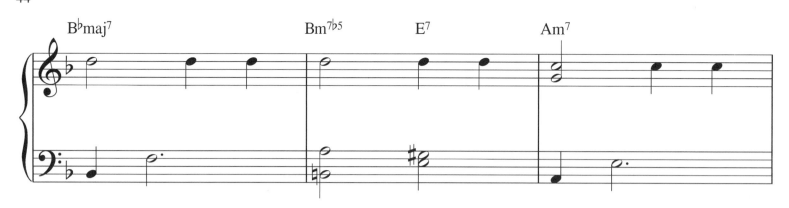

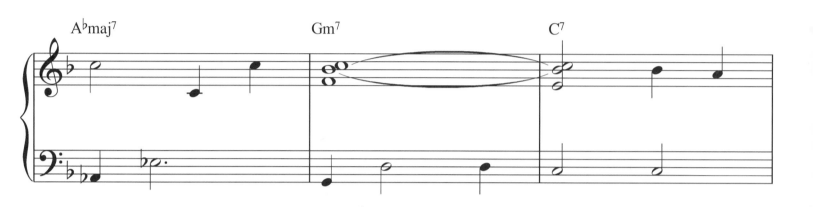

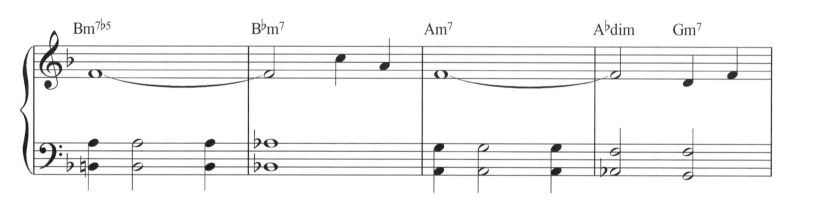

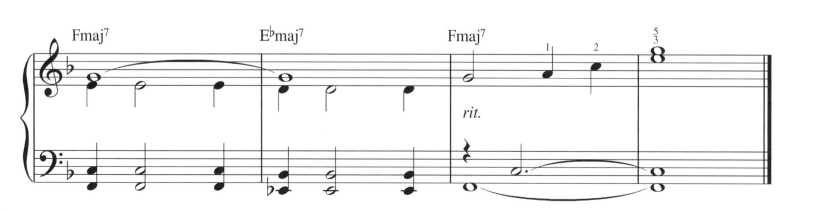

OH, GOOD GRIEF

By VINCE GUARALDI

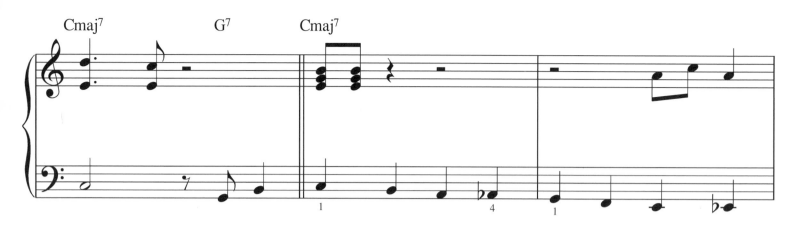

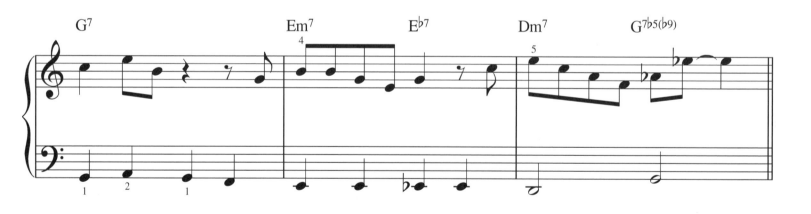

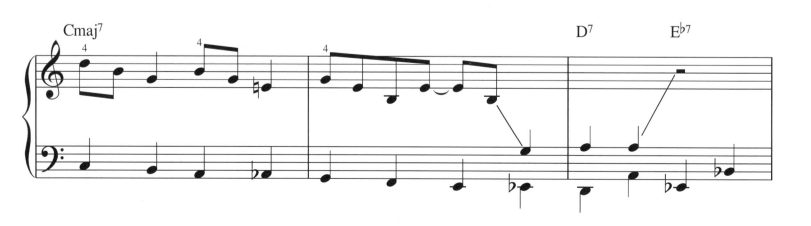

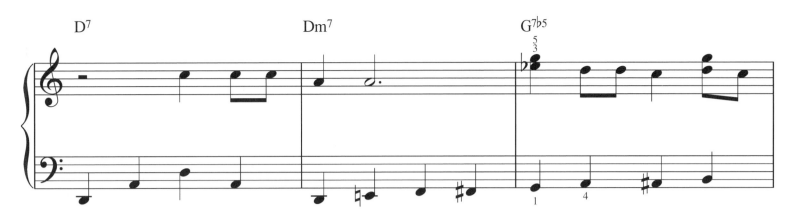

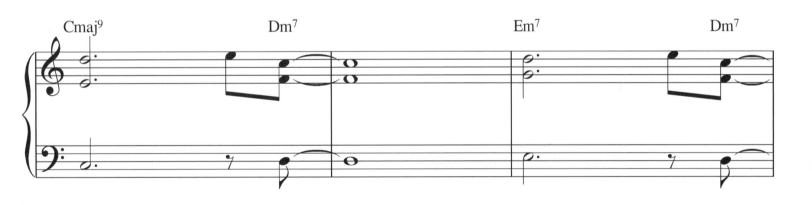

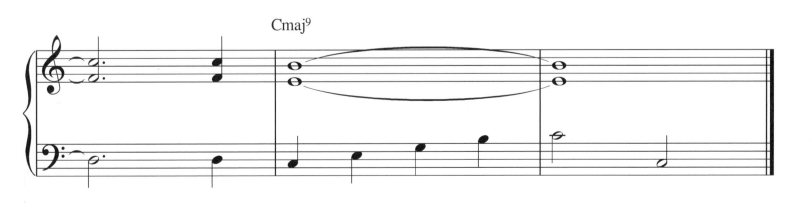

PEPPERMINT PATTY

By VINCE GUARALDI

Moderately bright

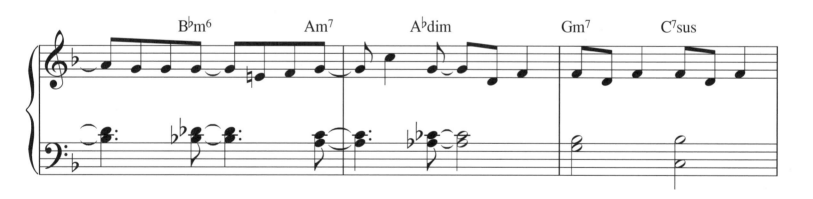

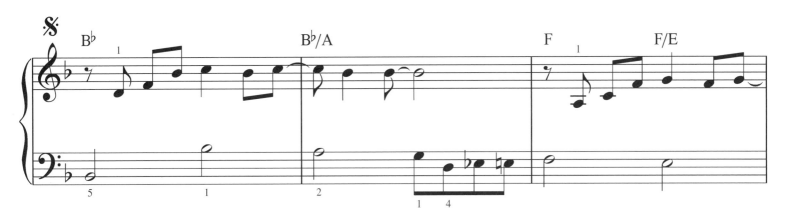

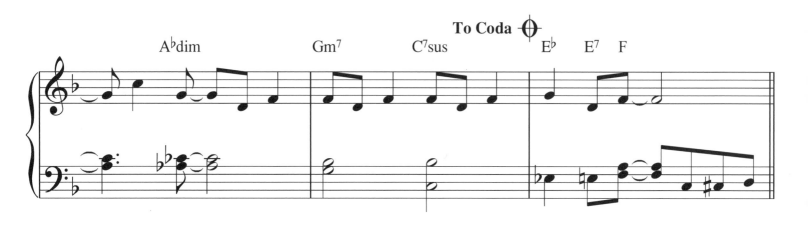

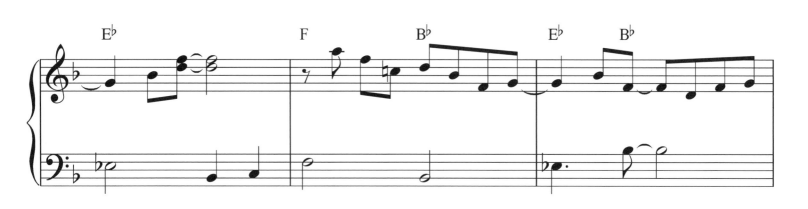

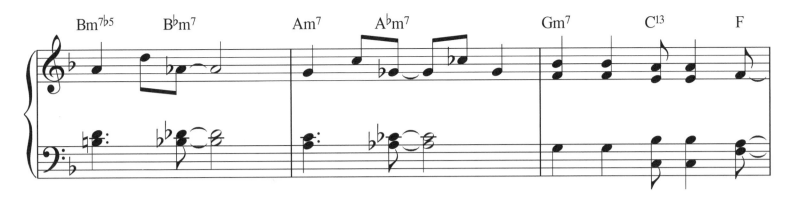

51

D.S. al Coda

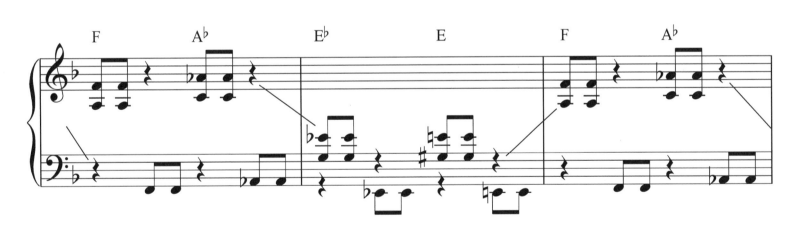

RAIN, RAIN, GO AWAY

By VINCE GUARALDI

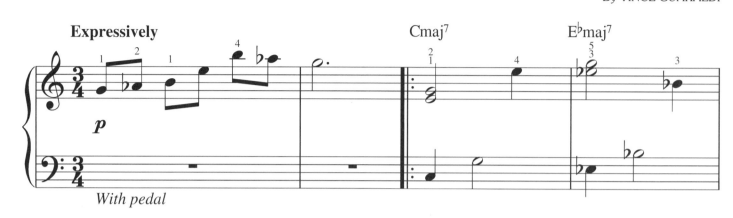

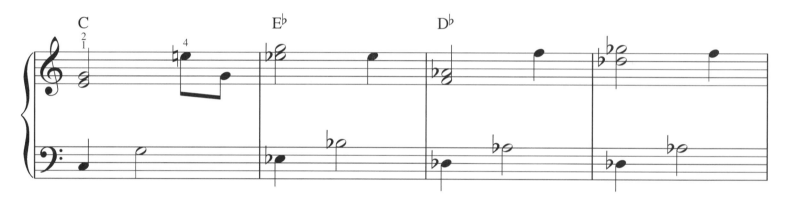

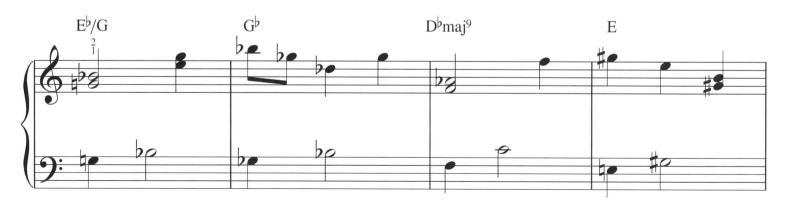

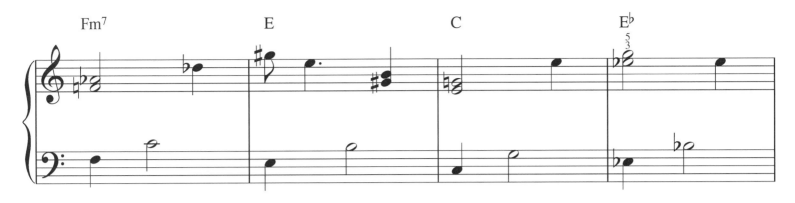

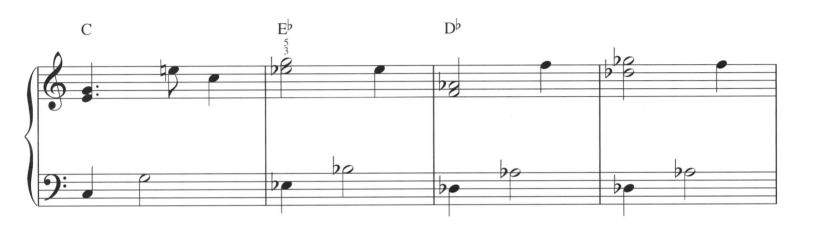

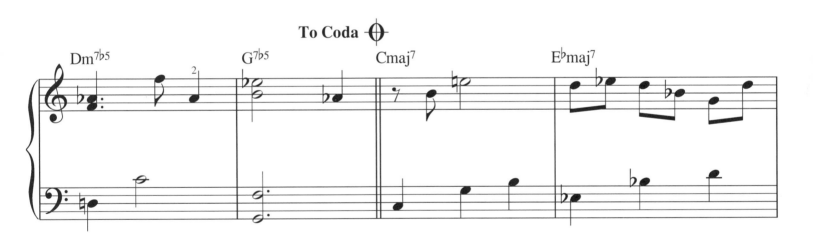

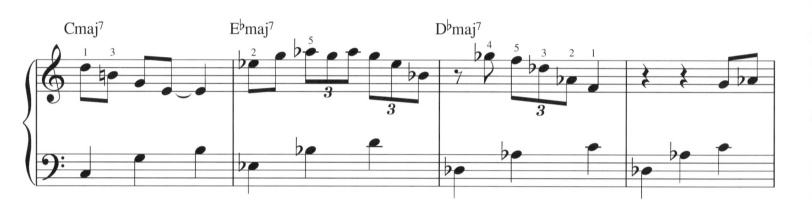

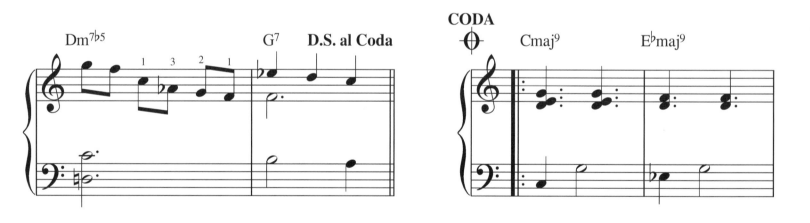

SCHROEDER

By VINCE GUARALDI

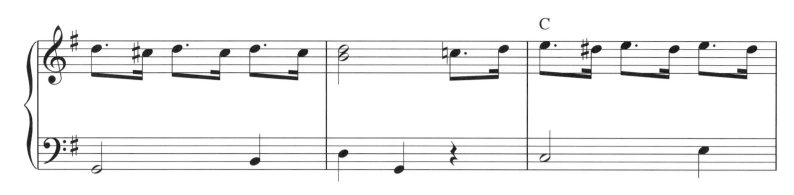

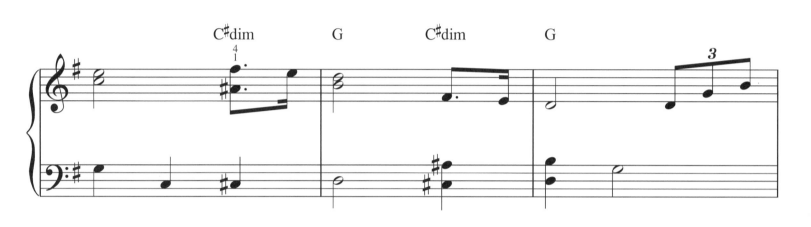

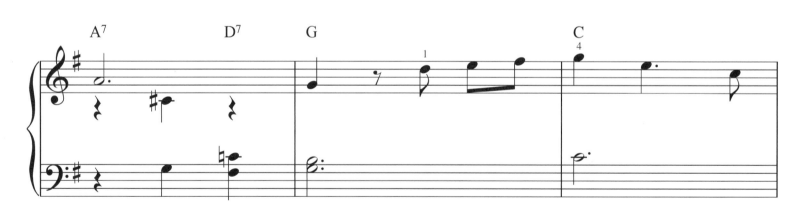

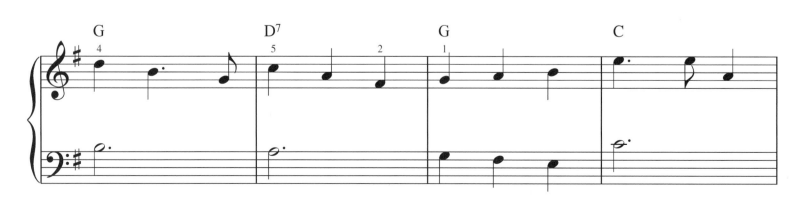

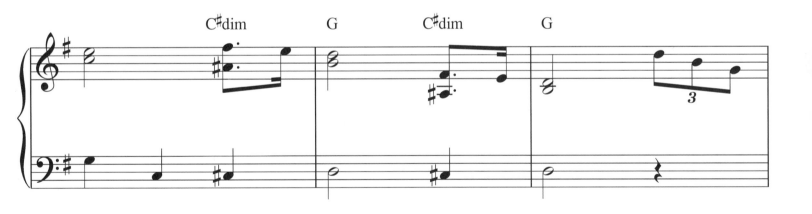

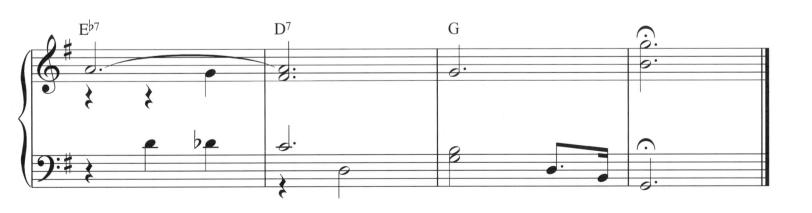

RED BARON

By VINCE GUARALDI

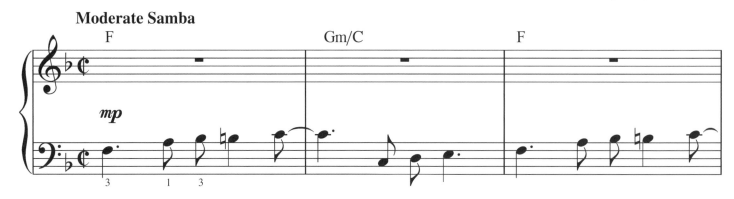

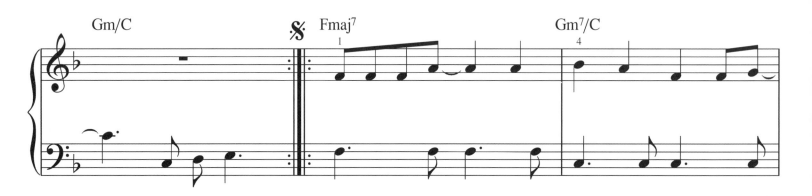

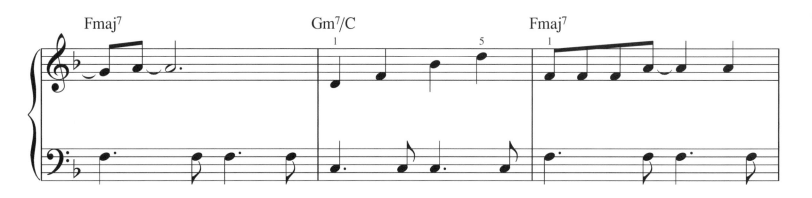

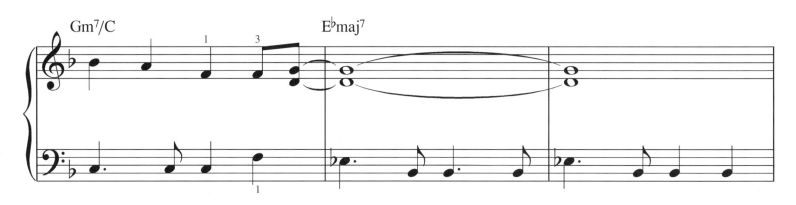

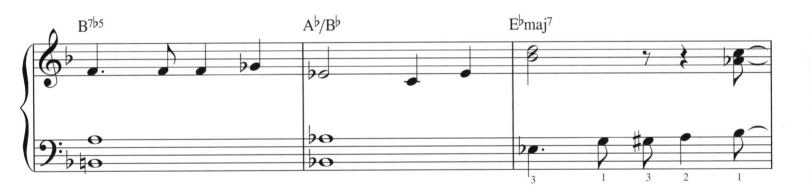

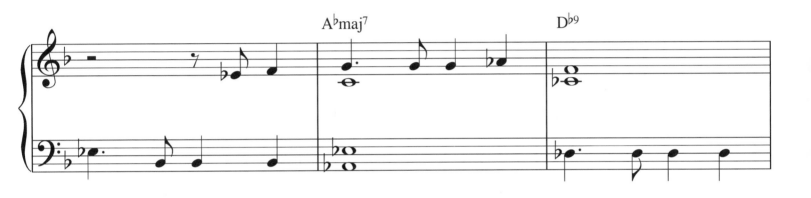

To Coda ⊕

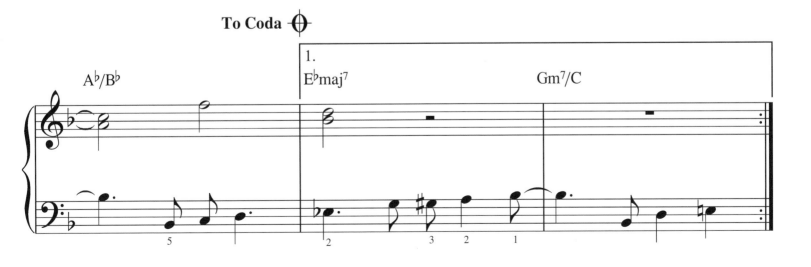

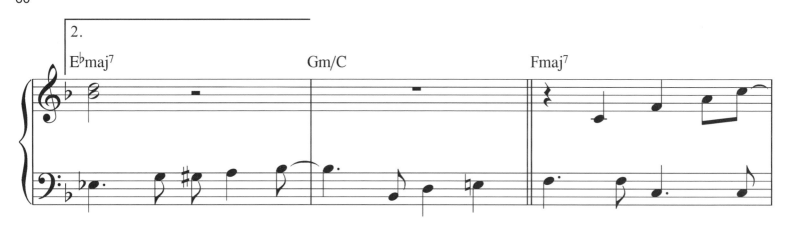

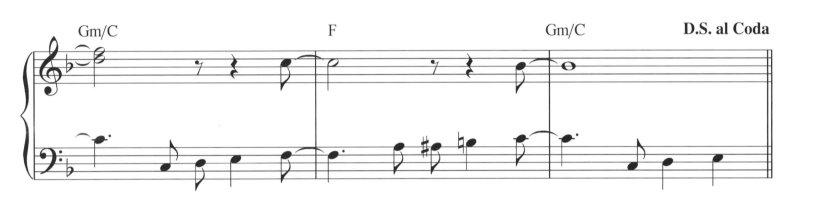

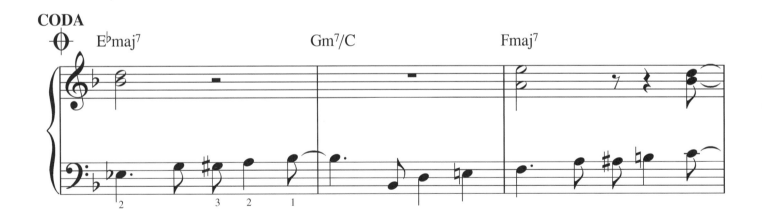

YOU'RE IN LOVE, CHARLIE BROWN

By VINCE GUARALDI

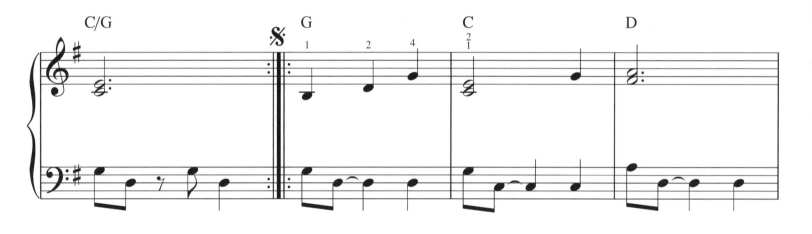

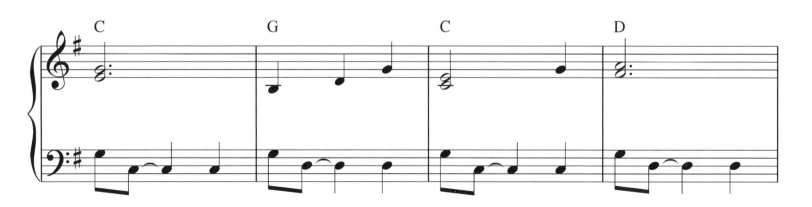

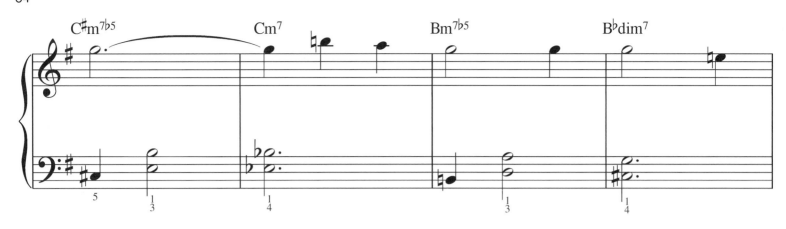

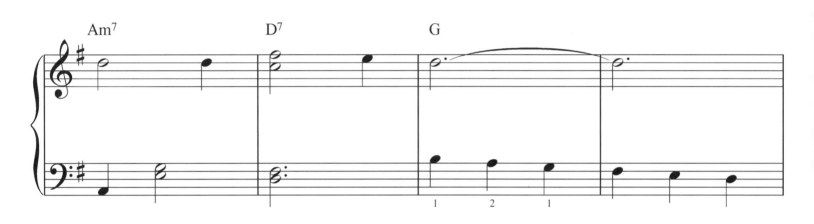

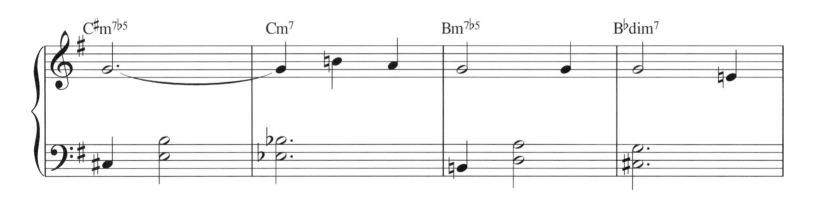

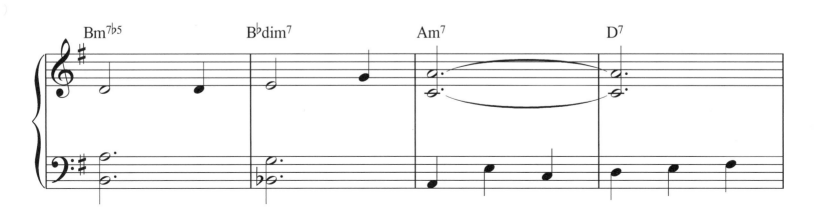

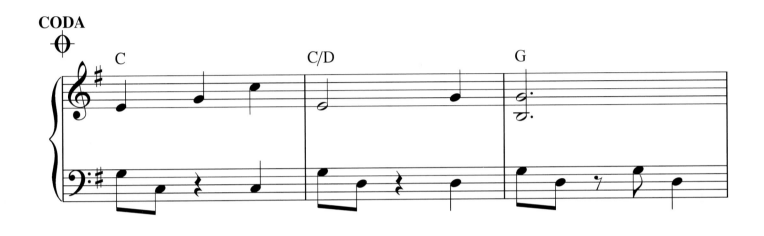

SKATING

By VINCE GUARALDI

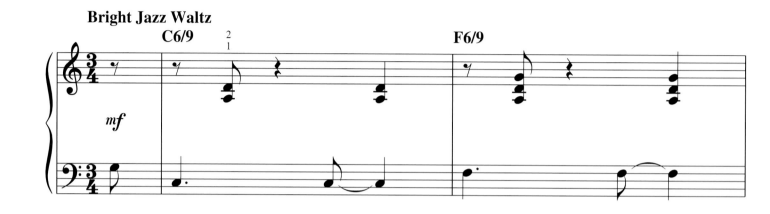

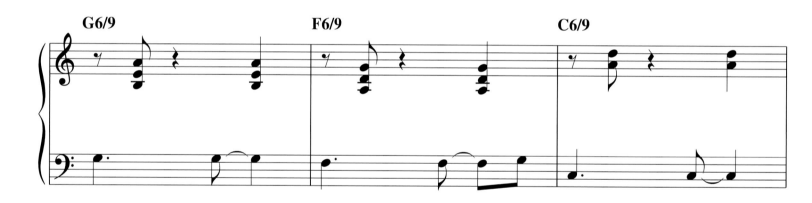

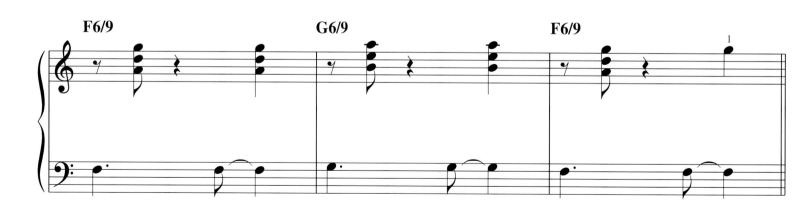

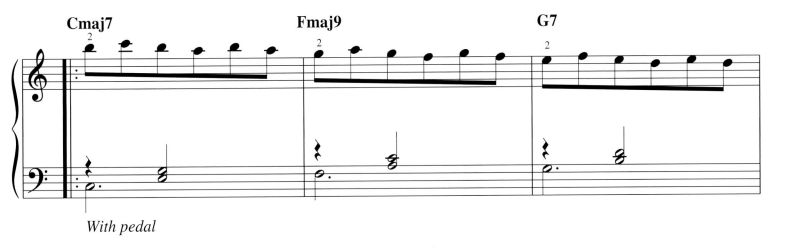

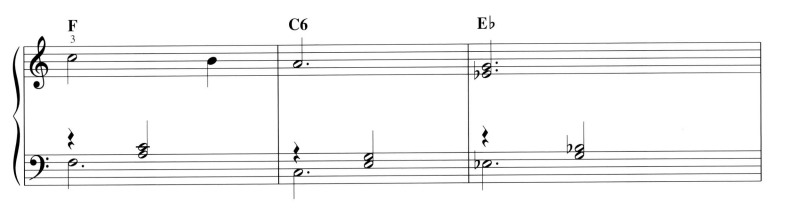

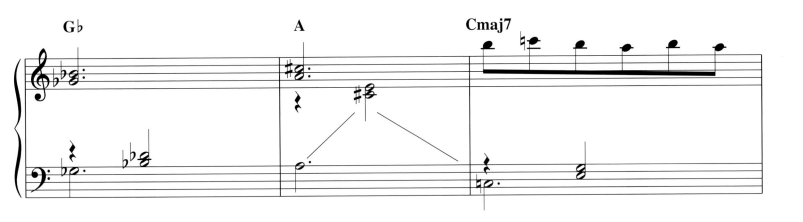

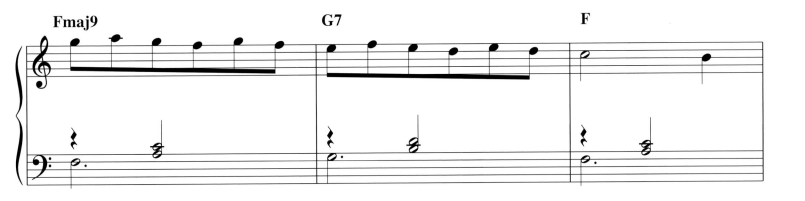

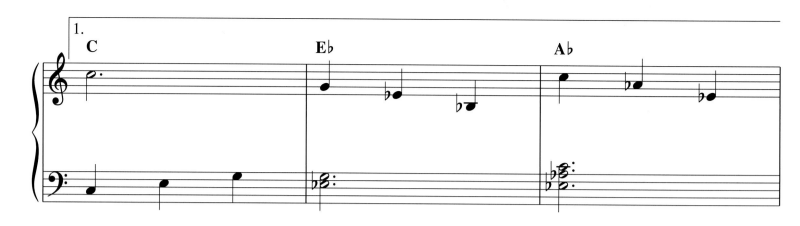

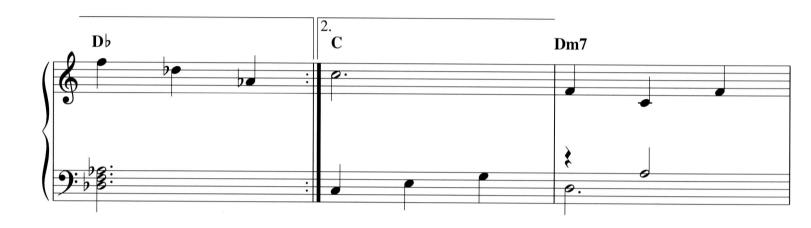

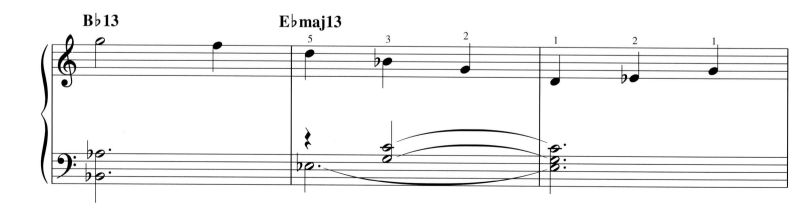

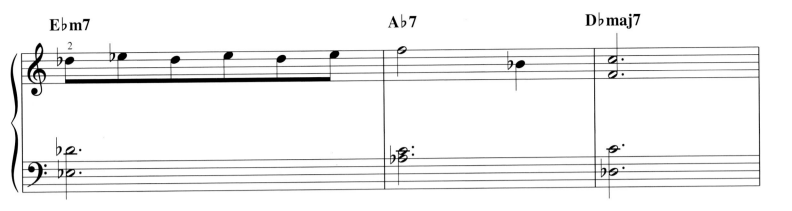

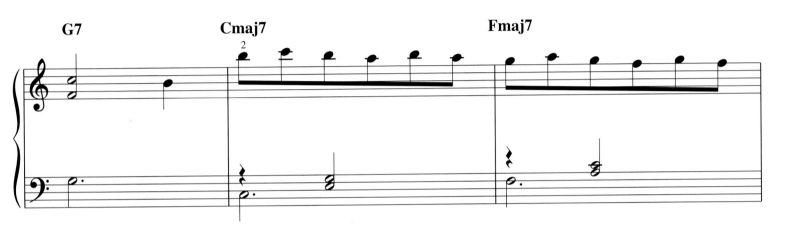

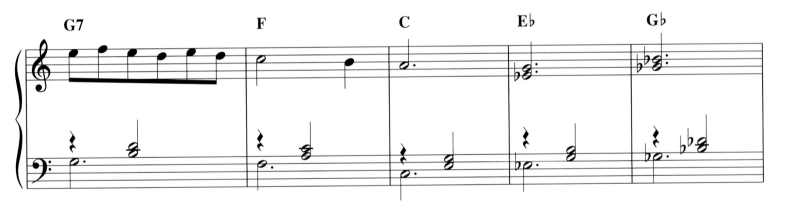

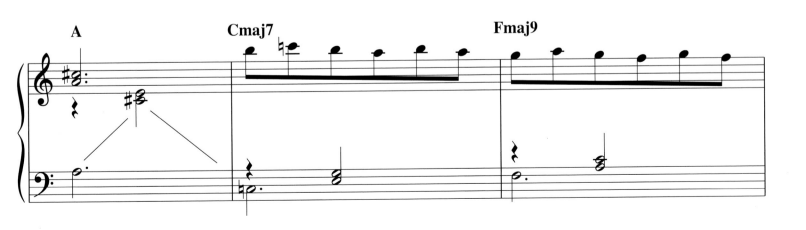

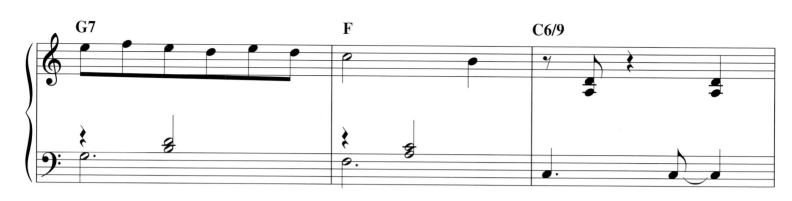

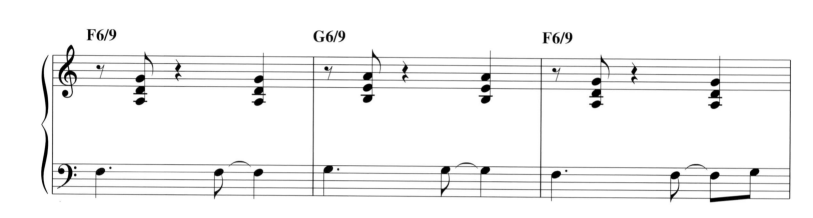

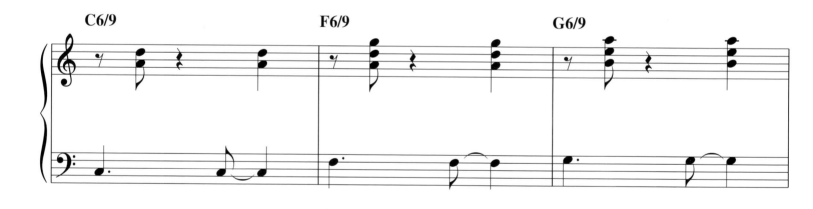

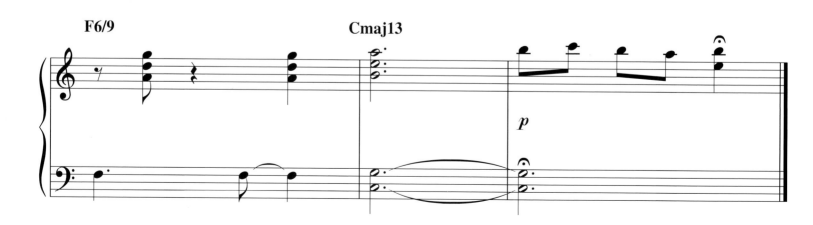